I0065273

Options Trading:

7 Golden Beginners Strategies to Start Trading Options Like a PRO! Perfect Guide to Learn Basics & Tactics for Investing in Stocks, Futures, Binary & Bonds. Create Passive Income Fast

Table of Contents

© Copyright 2018 by Mark Graham - All rights reserved.

The follow eBook is reproduced below with the goal of providing information that is as accurate and reliable as possible. Regardless, purchasing this eBook can be seen as consent to the fact that both the publisher and the author of this book are in no way experts on the topics discussed within and that any recommendations or suggestions that are made herein are for entertainment purposes only. Professionals should be consulted as needed prior to undertaking any of the action endorsed herein.

This declaration is deemed fair and valid by both the American Bar Association and the Committee of Publishers Association and is legally binding throughout the United States.

Furthermore, the transmission, duplication or reproduction of any of the following work including specific information will be considered an illegal act irrespective of if it is done electronically or in print. This extends to creating a secondary or tertiary copy of the work or a recorded copy and is only allowed with express written consent from the Publisher. All additional right reserved.

The information in the following pages is broadly considered to be a truthful and accurate account of facts and as such any inattention, use or misuse of the information in question by the reader will render any resulting actions solely under their purview. There are no scenarios in which the publisher or the original author of this work can be in any fashion deemed liable for any hardship or damages that may befall them after undertaking information described herein.

Additionally, the information in the following pages is intended only for informational purposes and should thus be thought of as universal. As befitting its nature, it is presented without assurance regarding its prolonged validity or interim quality. Trademarks that are mentioned are done without written consent and can in no way be considered an endorsement from the trademark holder.

Introduction

Congratulations on downloading *Options Trading for Beginners* and thank you for doing so.

The following chapters will discuss the best strategies that you can follow in order to get the most out of your own investing experience. Many people are searching for different methods they can use to help invest their money. They may choose to work in the stock market, to invest in real estate, to start their own business, and even put the money into retirement. Another choice that you can go with that has a lot of great strategies and can work no matter how the market is performing, is options.

With options, you are going to purchase the right to use the asset, rather than the actual asset. When the chosen expiration date occurs on that contract, the investor gets to choose whether they want to exercise their right to purchase or sell the underlying asset. And since this investment type is able to work no matter how the market is doing, it is the perfect choice when it comes to always being able to make money.

This guidebook is going to take a look at some of the basics that you need to know in order to get started with options trading. We will look at what options trading is about and some of the terms that you need to know to make the trading easier to handle. When that is done, we will explore some of the best strategies that you can utilize in order to really make a good profit from options trading, and how to limit your losses, how to invest in all market conditions, and so much more. Then we will end this guidebook with an overview of some of the methods you can use to limit your risks while maximizing your potential profits.

There are so many things to enjoy when it comes to options trading. When you are ready to get started with this investment type, make sure to check out this investment type and learn the best strategies and all the information that you need to see success.

There are plenty of books on this subject on the market, thanks again for choosing this one! Every effort was made to ensure it is full of as much useful information as possible, please enjoy!

Chapter 1: What is Options Trading?

Before we get into some of the strategies that come with options trading, let's take a look at the basics of stock options. You probably have a good idea of what a share or stock of a company is. To keep it simple, a single share is going to represent a solitary unit of ownership in that company. Companies will offer their shares for sale in order to raise some capital for themselves. These shares, or equities, are going to be listed as well as traded on the stock exchange amongst interested traders.

In the stock exchange, a lot of things can go on. You will notice that there are going to be many high profile shares that trade in huge volumes. These also may have some derivatives that are associated with them. A derivative is a contract that can occur between at least two parties, and sometimes more, in which the contract will derive its value from an underlying security, such as an index or a stock.

The most commonly traded derivatives that you are able to find on the stock market will be options and futures. We won't spend a lot of time on futures in this guidebook, but they are often easier to understand compared to options, but they often have less flexibility and will carry more risk with them.

An option, on the other hand, is going to be a type of contract, one that is sold by one party to another that will give the buyer the right, but not the obligation, to either sell or purchase an underlying stock at a pre-determined price. There is usually an expiration date or time that comes with these options and the buyer must decide what to do with it in that time frame. They can also choose to work with the underlying asset at any time before the expiration date occurs.

These options can't exist indefinitely and each of them has this expiry date. The option buyer will have the right to exercise their buyer at the time of the expiry, or they can use it before the expiry point. So, when would you want to use an option rather than relying on stocks?

One option is when you know that the price of the underlying option may go up in the future. You can purchase the option now, and then when the price does go up, you can exercise your right to purchase that stock at the lower price, and then sell it to make a profit.

A good example of this is when a land developer is waiting to hear if there will be some new regulations put in place on land. If the regulations or zoning rules do go into effect, the price of that land will go up. The land developer may enter into an options contract with the owner of the land. This gives them the right, but not the requirement, to purchase the land by the end of the expiry date that the two parties agreed upon. The land developer will have to put some money down as an incentive to the land owner to do the contract.

If the regulations do go through, then the land developer will agree to purchase the land at the reduced price. Their down payment will go towards the amount that they now owe. They never pay more than what the contract stated, no matter how much the land may be worth at the time of purchase. The land developer can now make homes in that area and sell them for a good profit because they got such a good deal.

There is some risk involved in this though. In the example above, if the regulations don't go through, the land developer may decide not to purchase the land. They don't have to go through and make the purchase, but they will have to forfeit the down payment that they made earlier so there is some monetary loss in the situation.

Types of options

When it comes to options, there are going to be two different types of options that you can work with. There will be the call options. These will give the buyer the right to purchase the underlying security of the contract at a fixed price. This would be like the example that we talked about above. There is also the put options, which includes options that give the buyer the right to sell the underlying security at a fixed price.

The biggest thing to remember here is that when working with the call option, the buyer of this option can only start to profit from that option if the value of the underlying stock or underlying index goes up. But in the other case with the put option, the buyer of the option can only start to profit when the value of the underlying stock or index goes down.

The benefits and the negatives of working with options

We have spent a bit of time taking a look at options and what they are all about. There will also be a ton of strategies that you are able to use when you decide to get into this kind of market and we will talk about them more as we go. But at this point, you may be wondering why a trader would be willing to start in the options market at all. It often seems more complicated than other forms of investing, and a new options trading investor may wonder if the risk is worth the profits in the long run?

There are a number of reasons why people would choose to work in the options market as their investment choice. First, an investor is able to profit on changes that occur in an assets price on the market, without ever having to put money up to purchase that equity. They do have to pay a premium on that, but they don't have to pay the full price of the asset in order to enter the market. The premium that needs to be paid is going to come in at a fraction of the cost of what the investor would pay if they bought that asset outright. This can help them to leverage their account more to get into a bigger trade, without having a lot of capital to start with.

Another benefit is that when an investor buys an options instead of just purchasing an equity, they are able to earn more per dollar that they invested compared to what they can do on the traditional stock market. This means that you have more potential profits than you would with traditional investing. But keep in mind that this also means there is more potential for losses with this trading as well.

Except when selling uncovered puts or calls, the risk that comes with options trading is going to be limited. When you purchase the option, the risk that you take on is going to be limited to the amount of premium that you were paying for the option, no matter how much the price of the stock moves against the strike price that you set.

With all of these benefits, it is a wonder why everyone doesn't decide to join the options trading market and use this as their investment tool to make a lot of money. But, just like with all the other investment types that you may try, options do have some main characteristics that will make a few investors turn away and look for other opportunities.

First, when you first enter into the market, you will find that these options are going to be time sensitive. A contract for an option is going to be for a short period of time, usually no more than a few months. It is also possible that as the buyer, you could lose all of your investment, even if you make a good prediction about which way the price moves and the magnitude of the price change. If the price change doesn't occur before the expiry date, you still lose out on your investment.

That time sensitivity can make it hard for a lot of people. It is a big risk to try and figure out the exact time frames for when certain actions are going to occur. If you are off by even one day, that means that you would lose out on the whole investment. But since these contracts can't be left for too long, and leaving them for longer than necessary can result in the stock reversing as well, this is a risk that many options traders have to deal with.

In addition, you will find that many investors consider options as a less tangible choice compared to the other investment types that you can choose. For example, if you purchase a stock, you will get a certificate that shows you own a part of the company. Even a Certificate of Deposit investment from the bank will do this for you. But as an investor in options, the purchase is going to be considered a book entry only investment. You don't technically own the asset that you are working with, you only own the contract and get the choice of exercising your right to purchase or sell that asset at a later time.

There are a lot of mixed reviews out there when it comes to options and how well they can be used for investment purposes. For some investors, these are the perfect vehicles to help them limit their risks a bit and increase the amount of profit that they are able to earn. For others, they are just too risky and they would rather find other, more safe, options that will help them to earn a good return on investment.

What is all comes down to is the fact that options and options trading just aren't the right fit for every investor. And just because you have heard of other people having success with options trading in the past doesn't mean that it is the right one for you. Options are going to be a risky type of investment, but they also provide you with a ton of opportunities to make a profit for investors who are willing to learn the ropes and

who will use this financial instrument to help
them make more money

Basic terms to know with options trading

Before we move into some of the information on
the different types of trades that you can do with
options and the strategies that will help you get
this done, we need to go through and look at
some of the basic terms that you should learn
about with options trading.

The strike price

Every contract that comes with options is going
to have a strike price associated with it. This is
going to be the fixed reference price against
which the settlement will take place at the time
the buyer exercises the option, or when the
expiration date of the option occurs. For any

given index or stock that is traded as an option, there will be different contracts that will correspond with the strike prices you and the seller choose. These will be pre-determined by the stock exchange in which that stock is traded.

In the case of doing a call option, this strike price is often going to be the buy price while the market price of the underlying stock functions as the sell price. This is going to be at the time of exercising the option or settling that option. In the case of a put option, the strike price is going to become the sell price and then the market price is going to become the buy price when it is time to exercise or settle the option.

The lot size

The lot size is going to talk about a fixed number of units of the security that you will cover with the options contract. The lost size is often going to be determined by whichever body is regulating the stock exchange, and sometimes there will be some variations between one stock and the next. These numbers will also be revised from time to time. If you are trading on the United Stated NYSE, then the standard lot size is going to be 100. This means that one options contract is going to allow the buyer to get 100 shares of that underlying index or stock.

The premium

The other term that you should know is the premium. This is going to be the amount of money that the buyer will pay, for each share, when they purchase an option. This can also be the amount of money that the seller will receive for each share when they sell an option. The premium that is offered for an option is going to vary based on different factors.

The expiry date

All options contracts will have expiry dates. Sometimes these dates will happen further into the future, and sometimes it will only last a few hours. Sometimes these dates will happen weekly, monthly, or even on a quarterly basis. These dates are often going to follow a pretty rigid calendar determined by whichever exchange the options are traded on. Both parties will be aware of the expiry date before any agreements are reached.

The buyer is going to have a few options here. They can choose to purchase the underlying asset before the expiry date, they can wait until right on the expiry date to make the purchase, or they can choose to walk away and not do the purchase at all. With the first two, the idea is that the buyer will get a good price on the underlying asset because they waited patiently. Now the price of that asset is higher and they can own it—and even sell it—while making a profit since they got it for such a good price.

Sometimes this doesn't work out as planned though, and the buyer may choose not to make the purchase. For example, if the stock isn't worth what they agreed upon price says, or it went way down in value, then the buyer may not exercise their right to purchase. In this case, the buyer will lose out on a little down payment that they had to give up, but at least they didn't have to pay the full price of the contract.

Now that we have a little better idea of what options are, why they can be useful, and some of the terms that are important with this kind of investment, let's start taking a look at some of the different strategies that you can use when trading in options contracts.

Chapter 2: The Bull Put Spread Strategy

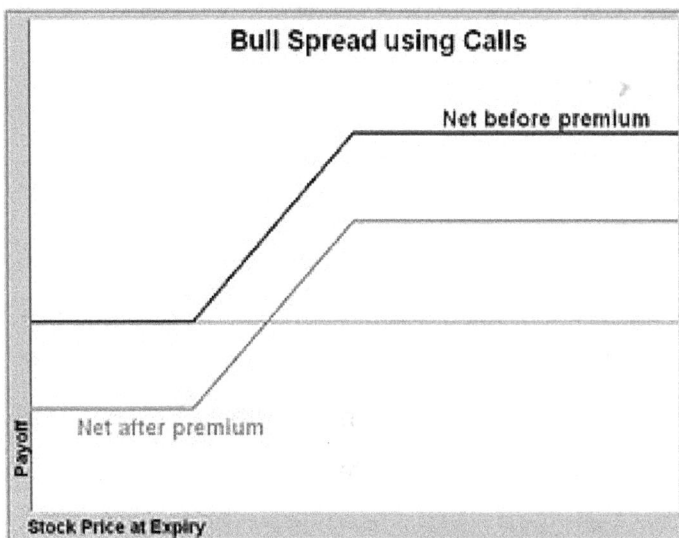

Bull Spread using Calls

Net before premium

Net after premium

Payoff

Stock Price at Expiry

The first type of strategy that we are going to take a look at is known as the bull put spread. This is considered a directional strategy that you can use any time the stock shows signs of reaching its support level, and it is believed that the stock price isn't going to fall down any further. At this stage, you will notice that the stock is either going to trade pretty flat, which means there isn't much movement in either direction, or it is going to start rising again. Since this strategy is a credit type spread, there are going to be two legs in this trade and the trader will be able to receive a net credit when they enter the trade.

How to execute this strategy

The first thing that you need to do for this strategy is to find an index or another stock that will fit the criteria for this strategy. You need to do a medium or short term outlook for the index and stock to make sure that it will meet these criteria. Once that is done, you will sell one OTM put option of that index or that stock. Then you can move on to purchase one OTM put option. This second one needs to have the same underlying index and stock as the other one, and the same expiry date, but the strike price needs to be lower.

Once you have been able to complete the steps above, you need to spend time monitoring that position continuously. You can then square off, or close, out both options at the same time once the trade has provided you with significant amounts of profit. You can also choose to hold onto the trade until the expiry of the options. This sometimes helps you to retain maximum profits. However, you should only do this if the stock doesn't seem to have a threat of falling under the strike price you had before the expiry date. Otherwise, you will lose out on all your profits.

When should I use this strategy?

You will want to trade on this kind of spread any time that you believe that your chosen index or stock has reached a really strong support level. You need to be confident that the stock or index won't go down any further from that level, at least before your expiry time.

A good time to get into this kind of trade is when the underlying index or stock is going some expected correction or some profit booking. Say that you see a stock that is fundamentally strong and it underwent a fair correction, where it declined by about five percent. Then, at the lower levels, this stock started to show some stability signs. You look at the charts and notice that the net buyers and the buying volumes were slowly increasing, which indicates that this particular stock is more likely to go up rather than down. That would be a good time to use this strategy to purchase a stock through an options contract.

In addition, you can choose to trade this when the stock is gradually making its way up and is showing signs that it won't fall in the near term. If you think that the price of the stock could fall at all before the expiry dates, then it is best to avoid this option at all costs because it will cost you a lot of money.

When using this kind of strategy, it is often preferable to trade options that have maintained a low level of volatility than others. You don't want a lot of big movements up or down with this strategy, because those lows can really harm your profits. It is best to have a stock that is pretty steady and doesn't show signs of moving quickly one way or another.

Sine this is considered a credit spread strategy, it is a good one to help you exploit time decay. This is because a price fall with a stock that has low levels of volatility is likely to be small and marginal, and therefore, it is unlikely to overcome the time decay of options. This can ensure that your trade stays profitable, even if your underlying asset starts to move away from your predictions. Of course, this rule isn't hard and fast and you can choose to pick some stocks that have higher levels of volatility too, as long as you take care to watch the stock and pick the right expiry dates.

Your potential for profits and loss

The amount of profit or loss that you will take with this strategy will depend on how much you paid, how much the market moved, and how big of lot size you purchased in the first place.

The way that you figure out the maximum profits you can make is, when you get to the expiry time, the stock price is trading above the strike price of your higher put option. The best way to figure out how much maximum profit you can get from this is going to be:

- Maximum profit = (premium received or selling higher-strike put option – premium paid for buying lower strike put option) X lot size.

The way that you can get the maximum amount of loss that you can suffer is when, at the time of your option expiry, the stock price falls below the strike price of the lower strike put option. The formula that you would use to find out this amount includes:

- Maximum loss = {(Difference of the two strike prices) – (Net premium received)} X Lot Size

Advantages and disadvantages of this option

The biggest advantage of using this type of strategy is that it can take the time decay that is usually an issue and make it work in your favor. Even if you don't see that underlying stock move up after it hits its support level, or if it stays stagnant, you can still gain a bit each day because of the time decay when you work with the bull put spread strategy. Also, if you end up trading during times of high volatility, any subsequent volatility drop is going to act as a type o catalyst that can make your trade more profitable than before.

One disadvantage that you may find with using this strategy is that the maximum profit that is there for this strategy is often much less than the amount that you could potentially lose on this trade. This can make it a riskier strategy to choose when you are a beginner.

Chapter 3: The Bear Call Spread Strategy

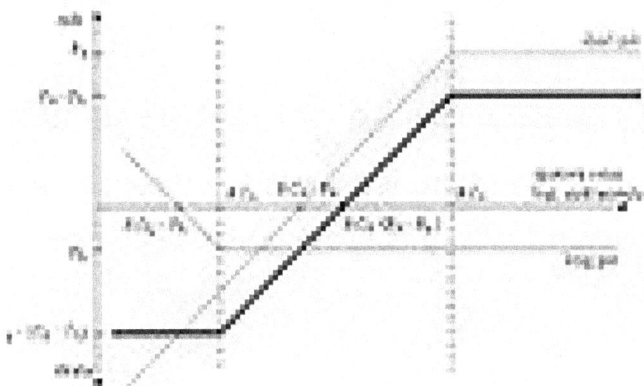

The next option that we are going to take a look at is known as the bear call spread. This is known as a directional strategy that the trader will use any time they believe that the underlying asset has reached its highest resistance level, and they believe that it is very unlikely that the price will go up much further. They believe in this strategy that the underlying asset is either going to stay flat or it will undergo a correction. Basically, this strategy is going to end up being the opposite of the strategy we did in the past chapter.

This is again a credit type spread. This means that the premium you will receive while selling one leg of the trade is going to be higher than the premium that you will pay when you purchase the second leg of this trade. This means that you will enter a net credit into the account when you do enter into the position.

Let's take a look at some of the things that you can do to get started with the bear call spread strategy. First, you need to go through and find the underlying asset that fits your needs and your criteria. You need to find an asset that is going to either stay flat or go down for the medium or short term. If you think that a stock may go even higher in value during your trading time, then this kind of strategy won't work for you.

Once you have chosen the stock that you would like to trade, you can sell the OTM call option of that chosen asset. Then you will go through and purchase an OTM call option, one that has the same underlying asset and expiry date as the ATM call option, but make sure that this second one has a higher strike price than the first.

While you are in the trade, you need to monitor it all the time, checking in at least once a day. You can then exit your position once you see that you are making a considerable profit. It is often recommended that you get out when the trade is going to make more than fifty percent of the max profit. If you feel that there is no risk of a reversal during the trade, then you can hold onto the trade until you reach expiry and then pocket the maximum profit.

One tip to follow here is that you should sell an OTM call option that has a delta value between 0.25 and 0.2 and having at least a month left for expiry. Then you can purchase an OTM call option that has two strikes greater than the sold call option. This helps you to retain a high (somewhere between 75 and 80 percent) probability of success while also allowing you to receive a substantial premium at the same time.

You can work with the bear call spread when you have a good reason to believe that your chosen underlying asset is unlikely to rise in the near term. You want to be confident that the asset is either going to decline or stay stagnant from its current price until the expiry date is done. For example, you may want to work with a stock that comes from a company where huge market expectations weren't met when the results were posted. In addition, if you are trading in index options, and you see that the index has hit a bit resistance level, this would be a good time to trade on a bear call spread.

Just like with the other option, you will not enter into this strategy if you see that the underlying asset has a lot of volatility. You want a steady stock that is going to either remain stagnant or one that is going to go down to make the most of this strategy. In addition, if you see that a rise in value with that stock is likely, then you would not want to invest either.

With this option, the maximum amount of profit that you are able to make using this strategy is going to occur when, at the time of its expiration, the stock price ends up trading below the strike price of the call option, with the lower strike price, that was sold.

You can also look for the maximum loss that is possible with the bull call spread. The maximum amount of loss that you will see from this strategy is going to be when, at the time of its expiration, the price of the stock starts trading above the strike price call option that you bought.

The advantages and disadvantages of using this strategy

As was the case with the bull put spread, the biggest advantage of using the bear call spread is that it can take the time decay issue and will make it work in your favor. As long as you can make sure that the stock stays below the lower strike price when you reach your expiry date, you will be able to keep the entire net credit that you were able to receive when you entered that trading position. This can be good news for traders who did their research and learned when the best times to enter the market were and picked out the best underlying asset to meet their needs.

The disadvantage of going with this position is if that underlying asset ends up making a sharp movement against expectations. The maximum amount that you could lose is going to be much higher than the potential maximum profit that you could earn in this trade.

Both the bear call spread and the bull put spread are going to work in a similar manner. But with the bear call spread, you want to find a stock that may not be doing as well. When you look at the charts, you want to look for one that has reached its resistance level and it looks like it will either stay stagnant with no movement or go down during the time of your trade. If you picked out the right underlying asset, then you will find that you can earn a profit from the trade you started.

You have to be careful with this one and take your time. Just because a stock has reached its resistance level doesn't mean that it is the right option for you to get into. There are many stocks that will go up above that resistance level, and if you chose to do this strategy with one of those assets, you would end up losing money on your trade. Take your time to really watch the market and that particular stock to make sure you are picking the right one.

Chapter 4: Condors and Butterflies Strategy

This chapter is going to take a look at both the condor and the butterfly strategy when it comes to options trading. Both of these are going to help you take advantage of a period of low volatility in the market, unlike some of the other strategies that we will discuss in this guidebook. Let's divide these up and get a better outlook on how both of these strategies can work.

The iron condor strategy

The iron condor is often going to be a combination of two vertical spreads; a bull put spread and a bear call spread. This strategy does provide you with four different options contracts, each going to have the same expiry dates, and they will have different exercise prices as well.

To make your own iron condor, you will need to sell an OTM all and an OTM put. At the same time, you would need to buy a further OTM call and then a further OTM put. Just like with the butterfly spread that we will talk about later, the iron condor is going to get its name from the diagram that comes with it, which basically resembles a big bird that has wings.

The main reason that any trader would want to work with this strategy, compared to some of the other low volatility strategies, is that it can allow you to get a bigger net credit, while still staying at the same amount of risk. However, the iron condor is going to come with additional costs because you will need to do more than one purchase and more than one sale to get this to work. Basically, this is going to have four legs of the trade, and you need to pay for each one, which can bring the initial costs up a bit.

What is the objective of working on the iron condor?

A trader who is looking at a stock and thinks that the price is not going to move much on that asset, and the ones who would like to limit their risks while trading will consider using this strategy. The benefit here is that it is generally going to allow you to earn a bigger premium while limiting how much they could potentially lose. The margin requirement that is there to help support your position is going to be limited to one single spread, which makes it easier to get a higher potential return on the investment.

The nice thing about working with the iron condor is that it is a limited risk, but also a limited profit strategy that benefits when there is a low amount of volatility in the underlying security while you keep this strategy open. You will be able to maximize your potential for profit by looking at the credit received at the outset of constructing the position and it is earned if your chosen asset doesn't move far from its original course by the end of your expiration date.

A loss on this strategy would happen if the chosen assets price didn't move at all, or if it ended up closing outside of the strikes that you set. The maximum that you can potential lose is going to be calculated when you look at the difference between the prices you chose for either spread. Then you would multiply that by the size of the contract and subtract the premium that you received at the beginning of the trade.

Being able to understand the maximum profit that you can potentially make, as well as the potential loss, can be crucial when you work on this strategy. The strategy is not going to make you a huge profit, but you can make some and it does reduce your risks a bit. While the potential loss that you may deal with is larger than the profit potential, there is a cap on how much you can lose, which will really help when you want to reduce your risks.

In addition, depending on how you decide to construct the iron condor, it is possible that you could go through and increase how probably it is that you would have a profitable trade, though this would be at the expense of profit potential. So, there are different ways that you could do this, and the method that you choose will make a big difference in how much profits and losses that you will deal with n this trade.

With this kind of strategy, the proper strike prices will be so important when it comes to how successful you will be when using the iron condor. You need to fully understand what trade-offs occur between the probability of success and the maximum profit potential that you may reach. Traders of this strategy will seek to position the strike prices of the sold part close enough that they will get a higher credit, but still far enough apart that there is a strong probability that the underlying asset will settle between the two when you reach your expiration date.

When you are able to keep this range as narrow as possible, a trader will sometimes reduce how likely they are to be successful. The further that you can move those prices, the higher the probability that you will have success with the trade.

Working with the butterfly spread

Another option that you can work with is the butterfly spread. These choices are designed to profit from volatility levels that are different all the time. If you work with a long call butterfly spread, you will earn a profit when the volatile stays low and you feel like the stock will stay pretty steady without much movement while you hold onto the contract. In order to create one of these spreads, you would purchase one ITM call option contract, making sure that the strike price remains low, purchase one OTM call option with a strike price is higher, and then you would sell two ATM call option contracts where the price is going to be somewhere in the middle.

The reason that this is known as a butterfly spread instead of another name is because the profit/loss diagram, which appears to have wings and a body. We are going to spend our time here looking at the long call spread. You can also do a short butterfly spread as well, which can be constructed by taking the opposite positions of what we will talk about with the long call and it is designed to help the trader profit when the volatility of the stock is going to increase in the future.

The objective of doing this kind of spread is to let the price of the underlying asset end up at, or at least near, the middle strike price when you reach your expiration time. This means that you are making the prediction that the asset is going to keep with a low amount of volatility and that it will just move inside a small range. The strike price of these options will be where the maximum potential profits could be found. However, the potential loss is going to be limited to the cost of creating this strategy.

The profit potential percentage is then going to be relative to the amount of funds that you need to start the trade; the amount that this comes in at can be really attractive. Also, the risk is going to be capped if you see that your prediction was wrong and the market ends up moving sharply up or sharply down.

The biggest disadvantage that can come with this strategy is that there is the possibility that you could be wrong with your predictions. The market could move up or down sharply and you will end up with a loss in the long run. You will also see that the potential trading costs versus the limited amount of potential for making a profit can be high.

There are a lot of variations that can come with this kind of strategy. These variations are going to be designed to help the trader profit based on high levels of volatility in the market. It is also possible for you to create a butterfly spread that has a put option, rather than the call option that we talked about before. The long call butterfly spread is also an option that you can choose that will help you to take advantage of your forecast in an environment that sticks with low amounts of volatility.

There are times when the market is going to be more volatile, and times when the stock price will seem to stay pretty steady and not move all that much. You want to make sure that you are able to trade in options during these different times, while still being able to make a profit along the way.

Both the iron condor and the butterfly spread can be great options to help you reach your goals. They can deal with all sorts of volatility in the market, and you can choose to either do a call or a put on the trade based on where you think the market will go. It is important that you take the time to look through your various charts and graphs, and do some research into the news that would affect the price of the stock. This will make a big difference on where you set the strike price, how you will enter the market, and how much in profits and losses you can potentially make with your trade.

Working with the iron condor and the butterfly spread can work when you don't expect a big increase or decrease in the price at all. These are usually pretty short term; you don't need to pick out a stock that never moves at all. But if it looks like a stock has kept away from a lot of volatility, and you don't think there is going to be a big news event that can mess with the value of the stock, then it is a good idea to go with these strategies.

Chapter 5: The Long Strangle and the Long Straddle Strategy

Now we are going to take a look at the long straddle and long strangle strategies and how they are similar and different. We will take a look at the long straddles first. Long straddles can be nice because they provide you with an opportunity to earn unlimited profits on your trade while taking away a lot of the risk that comes with options trading. You will want to choose the long straddle strategy when you see that your chosen underlying asset is going to experience quite a bit of volatility in the near term, or at least during the term that you plan to invest in the option for.

Out of all the strategies that we are going to discuss in this guidebook, the long straddle is often the riskiest, and many times it is the strategy that only experienced investors are going to spend their time on. In many cases, it is the strategy that should only be used in really rare situations when the trader notices some huge price movement, or when a huge price movement is expected in the near term for the underlying asset.

With that being said, the long straddle is also the strategy that can bring in the most potential profits compared to the other strategies in this guidebook. That is because the long straddle, unlike some of the other strategies that we have discussed, doesn't have an upper limit, or a maximum, on how much profit you can earn.

Right now, we are just going to focus on the long straddle, but the long strangle is a similar strategy that is just modified a little bit to help take out some of the risks. We will spend more time talking about that strategy a little bit later in this guidebook.

To start with the long straddle, you need to go look through your charts and find either an index or a stock that will fit all the criteria for trading on this strategy. We are interested in the short-term outlook for that asset right now. With the long straddle, you need to find an asset that has a lot of volatility in the short term, so find an option that has a lot of up and down movement and seems like it will keep up with that right now.

Once you have found the asset that you want to work with, you will start out by purchasing an ATM call option for that asset. Second, go and purchase an ATM put option. You want to have them with the same expiry date and the same underlying asset that you chose with the first option.

As soon as you enter into the trade, make sure that you monitor the option closely. You want to watch out for a big price movement to take place. Once that happens, you will close out both parts of the trade at the same time and take your profits. Since you will notice that time decay can impact both of these options, it is not a good idea to hold onto the long straddle for more than a few days. If you enter this trade, you want a lot of volatility with some signs that a breakout is going to occur (either an uptrend or a downtrend) so that you won't get stuck with a loss.

The strike prices that come with the call and put options need to be the exact same in this kind of strategy. However, when you enter into a trade, it is not always possible to buy the options when the market price of the stock exactly matches the strike price that you choose. The amount may be slightly higher or lower, but try to keep them as close as possible for this. If you have to, you can also slightly OTM one and then ITM the other when starting the trade to get the results you want.

The long straddle and the long strangle trade are only going to be used on rare occasion, usually when you see that a sharp and sudden rise or fall in the stock is going to happen. This will often happen when an external factor starts to push onto the stocks and makes the supply and demand change. When you enter into this position, you also need to make sure that the volatility isn't too high, usually staying less than 60 percent of historical volatility. This is because if you see a sharp drop in the volatility, even after the price movement of the stock occurs, the drop is going to end up cutting into your profit potentials on this kind of trading strategy.

This is a strategy that can be ideally traded any time there is a big decision or policy that would have an impact on the underlying stock. Any decisions that a company makes could cause this volatility to occur, so in addition to watching the graphs for the stocks, you also need to pay attention to the news about these stocks. The movement may be up or down based on the news and how investors react to it.

Some of the different situations where you would want to trade with the long straddle include:

- When the quarterly or annual results of a company are due within the next few days, and the investors have huge expectations from it.
- When a major decision that will influence the future of the company is due to come out in the next few days. Examples of this would be a change in who leads the company or changes in management, or a decision on a merger.
- When a major announcement on a large dividend or a bonus issue is imminent.

If the underlying is more like a benchmark index, there are times when different situations will create a big fall or rise. This may include events like the announcement of the annual financial budget, big policy decisions concerning money, major election results within the company, and major socio-economic decisions.

You do not want to trade with the long straddle if the underlying asset is trading in a narrow range. You also want to avoid this strategy if the index or stock stays pretty neutral for the short term. You can also avoid the long straddle if the implied volatility is high, even if there is some good potential for movement at some point.

If you are in a long straddle position, you will want to exit the position as soon as you see that the sharp fall or rise happens and you earn a profit. If you end up holding onto the position for too long after you make a profit, you an easily risk your profits due to the volatility, time decay, or both.

The main advantage of using this long straddle strategy is that it can help you earn potentially unlimited profits once the trade crosses your breakeven point in either of the directions. This one is set up so that you can earn whether the volatility goes up or down, so if the option does end up going with a sharp up or down, you can earn a profit from it. However, you should make sure that you leave the trade at a reasonable time.

While there is the potential to earn unlimited profits, this doesn't mean that you should keep on going forever. At some point, that sharp turn in either direction is going to give in, and the stock will stagnate or go the other way, making you lose out on your profits. Leaving once you earn a decent profit, rather than holding on and hoping that you can make even more, can ensure that you actually get to take some profits with you.

Another advantage of the long straddle is that you can use it to earn some profits in a market that is volatile, without having to try and make predictions on which direction the stock is moving. Since you are able to make some profits from the rise and the fall of your underlying asset, you will not have to worry about which direction the stock or index will head.

And the final advantage of this option is that all the risk exposure that you will run into is going to be limited. Your risk is only going to be the amount of premium that you paid at the time that you entered the trade.

Now, there are some disadvantages that can come with this trading option. The first issue with the long straddle trade is that it does have to deal with time decay. And since the time decay can affect both legs of the straddle that you are dealing with, the time decay issue can become compounded. This means that you will have to move quickly with your trades to avoid running into this problem along the way.

Another disadvantage that a trader may notice is that in order to earn a profit from the strategy, there needs to be a very sharp movement of your underlying asset and that sharp movement needs to happen very quickly. This has to happen so that you can still earn a profit and you can beat off the issues that come with time decay.

The long strangle

Now it is time to talk about the long strangle. This strategy is going to be similar to what we talked about with the long straddle. This one will allow you to buy a slightly OTM call and a slightly OTM put instead of the ATM call and put that we discussed earlier. You will need to make sure that you are using the same expiry dates and the same underlying asset to make the long strangle strategy work for you.

The advantage of doing the long strangle strategy instead of the long straddle is that the total premium that you will need to pay to get into this position is going to be lower than the amount of the long straddle. This can lower your risks in some cases, but since the long strangle needs a bitter move to help you recover your costs so you have to choose which one makes the most sense for the situation that you are in.

It is possible to profit from the long Strangle when you see that there is a sharp move by the stock. This is similar to what you see in the long straddle, but remember that the amount of the move and how quickly it occurs is going to be greater when you are working with the long strangle. In addition, your potential profits are potentially unlimited.

There is still a chance to receive a loss when you are working with the long strangle, so you need to weigh your risks with the potential profits and see whether you want to go with the long strangle or with the long straddle. A maximum loss is going to be incurred if the stock price ends up settling between the call strike price and the strike price of the put at the time of expiry. The maximum loss, just like with the long straddle, is going to be the amount of premium that you paid to buy the call and the put options when you first got started with this trade.

At this point, you may be curious as to which strategy, either the long straddle or the long strangle, that you would want to work with on a trade. It often depends on the market and how big of a sharp movement, either up or down, you think is going to be there.

If you think that the movement will be sharp in either direction, but you don't think it is going to be a very large one, then the long straddle is the best option to choose. It may cost a bit more with premiums but allows you to have shorter strike prices so you are able to earn a profit with that movement.

If you think that there is going to be a rather large price movement either up or down, then you may want to consider going with the long strangle for your investment option. This one will cost you a lot less, and you can earn a profit if your investment actually has the large movement that you think it will have. The trick is to follow the market and know what is going to occur with a stock based on various factors. Never just jump in and assume that you are going to get either of these to work for you. Research the market, study the graphs, and decide what is going to work the best for your needs.

Chapter 6: The Bear Put Spread Strategy

Setting-up a Bear Put Vertical Spread
(c) OptionPundit.com

Current stock price $50.00

Buy 1 put - $48.00 strike price

Sell 1 put - $46.00 strike price

Jan 18th ———— Jan 31st - expiration date

Another strategy that you can choose to work with is known as the Bear Put Spread. This is a directional strategy and one that the trader would use when there is a negative outlook on their chosen asset. When they expect that the asset is going to fall moderately over the next few months, the Bear Put Spread Strategy is the one that they would choose to work with. This is also a debit spread strategy, which means that you will need to pay in a net debit so that you can enter into this position.

So, like with the other strategies, the way that we start this one is to find the perfect index or stock that will fit the criteria to trade on this strategy. Remember that we want to find a stock or an asset that is likely to go down a little bit over the short term. If the asset that you are looking at is going to head up in value or stay stagnate, it is difficult to earn any profits with this strategy. So, make sure to look through the different charts and graphs that are available, and pick an underlying asset that looks like it will fall a bit while you are in your chosen position.

Once you have the underlying asset that you want to use picked out, it is time to buy one slightly OTM put option. Next, you can sell one OTM put option that has a strike price below the option that you bought above. You want the strike price to be about one or two strikes lower, you can choose based on the amount of risk that you want to take on. Make sure that both of these have the same underlying asset with them, and that they are both going to expire on the same date for this to work.

After you have entered the market, make sure to monitor the position on occasion. You will want to square off with both options once you see a significant amount of profit from the trade. It is often recommended that you square off this when you reach about thirty to forty percent of your maximum potential profit. If you think that the stock will continue to go down, then you can stay in for a bit longer, but watch out because the trend could reverse, and you will lose out on profits.

One thing to note is that as with the Bull Call Spread—which we will talk about later—if you increase the spread, you are then able to increase the amount of profit that you could potentially make. Doing this can earn you more money, but it also comes with more risk. You can also choose to decrease the spread, which reduces the risk and can reduce how much potential maximum profit you would earn on that trade.

You will want to work with the Bear Put Spread when you see that the market has a negative outlook on the stock. This can happen when you see a market that has a pretty negative outlook on the stock when there is some development, such as a below par earnings result. Sometimes this can be when there is any organization changes or decision making in the company, that is seen as a negative thing by the investors. You may also look at doing this kind of trade when a particular sector, the company is part of, is under some selling pressure. This often happens because of some unfavorable market or environmental conditions that have just been released.

This is another one of the debit spread strategies, which means that time decay is going to work against you. This means that you need to really watch any times when the value of the stock seems to go up or stagnates. Even if the value doesn't go up, the time decay can make it so that you lose out on money. This is a lower issue than using the naked long put position, but it is still something that you need to watch out for.

To figure out how much potential maximum profit that you could earn with the Bear Put Strategy, when you get to the time of expiry, you want the stock to be trading below the strike price of the lower strike put option. To figure out the potential maximum loss that you could encounter with this strategy when the price of the stock is at the expiry date, it ends up being above the strike price of the higher strike put option.

When you look at the advantages and disadvantages of this method, you will see that this spread is going to be similar to what we will see in the Bull Call Spread. To start, the primary advantage that you will run into is that this trade can be a good one when you want a good reward to risk ration and a moderate down move by the stock. Both of these can yield you some good profits if you get out of the market before the time decay becomes a big problem.

You are also able to increase the amount of potential profits that you can get with this spread by widening the spread. This basically means that you can increase how much you can potentially earn in profits by increasing the strike prices between the two options you purchase, but this will also increase the amount of risk that you take. Or, you can limit your risks a bit by decreasing the spread or lower the number of strike prices that occur between the two options that you purchase.

The main disadvantage that comes with this strategy is the time decay that we talked about before. The time decay is going to work against the position and even though there might be a limited loss potential, if you see that the stock or index stays stagnant for a long period of time, you will have to close out the position at a loss. This is why it's so important to watch the trade and make sure that things work the way that you were planning with it.

The strategy is a great one to work with any time that you see the market is going to move downward moderately. It is also a good example of how options can allow you to make money in the market, even if an economic downturn is going to happen. You should be wary of picking out the right stocks and ensuring that they will maintain their downward trend for the time that you are in the trade and watch out for the issues that can show up in terms of time decay, or you may easily end up with a loss when you close out your position.

Chapter 7: The Bull Call Spread Strategy

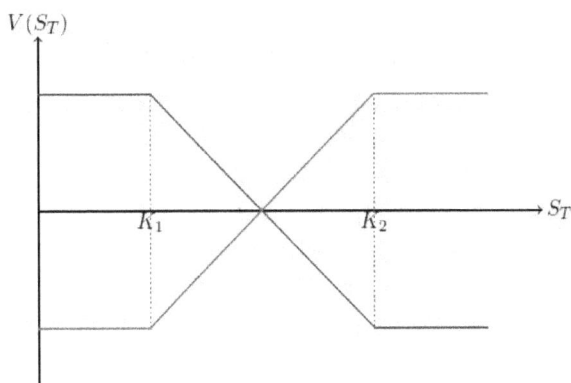

Figure 3.9: Red: Bull spread call. Blue: Bear spread call

The next strategy that we will look at is known as the bull call spread. This is another of those directional strategies that can be used any time that the trader has a positive outlook on that underlying asset, and they think that there will be a moderate amount of increase in price over the short term.

As it was with any of the other spread based strategies that we discussed, both the potential losses and potential profits are going to be capped when you use the bull call spread. However, one of the benefits of using the bull call spread instead of one of the other strategies is that the maximum profit that you could potentially earn from this strategy is going to be above the maximum loss that you can incur. In fact, there is a fair margin between the two, which means that your risk is much lower.

Unlike with the other strategies that we have discussed, this strategy is going to be a debit spread. This means that you are going to need to pay in a net debit before you are able to enter into the position. The Bull Call Spread, as well as the Bear Put Spread, are the two directional strategies that can provide you a high percentage of returns because you are able to use these in order to capitalize on directional momentum while still keeping the risk that you take on pretty low overall.

The next thing that we need to take a look at is how to execute this strategy. The first idea is to take a look at finding the perfect underlying asset that meets all of your criteria for working on this strategy. You want to have an asset that has a pretty positive outlook and will rise moderately while you hold onto it and before your expiry date.

Once you have found the asset you want to work with, you should first purchase one slightly OTM call option. Then you can sell one OTM call option, but make sure that its strike price is one or two strikes higher than the option that you first purchased. You want to make sure that you are using the same underlying index and stock and that this comes with the same expiry date as well.

When you enter into this market, you need to make sure that you check in on the position periodically from when you scheduled it to the expiry date. You will then want to close out both of the positions once your trade is able to yield you a significant amount of profit. This will usually be when the profit reaches somewhere between thirty to forty percent of the maximum potential profit that is possible.

You will want to work with the Bull Call Spread when you see that the market has a positive outlook on the stock. This can sometimes happen after a positive development is released about the stock, such as earnings results that were good. It may also include some strategic move by the company that can help increase its growth, whether this growth will happen right away or in the near future. You may also consider using the Bull Call Spread on any stocks that have been overcorrected and look like they are going to show some strong signs of going through a reversal.

One thing to note with this method is that because you are working with a debit spread strategy, time decay can work against you in this one. This is true even if the decay is slower than with a naked long call position. In many cases, it is not a good idea to hold onto this kind of spread for over two weeks, unless you can see that the position is continuously gaining at the end of two weeks, and you expect that there is going to be a lot more positive movement soon.

If you are in this kind of trade and the stock you chose is showing no momentum for more than two weeks when you are in this strategy, you should exit the position. This is true even if you end up with a small amount of loss. This frees up your capital to use on other trades. Some traders assume that the market will turnaround if they just stay in a little longer. But doing this keeps your capital stored and unusable, and there is the potential that the trade will go opposite of what you want, and this can cost a lot of money.

The maximum profit that you will be able to make with the Bull Call Spread will occur when, at the time of expiry, the stock ends up trading about the strike price of the call option that was done at the higher strike call option. Then the minimum loss is going to be incurred in this strategy when the price of the stock, when it gets to its expiry, is below the strike price of the lower strike call option you chose.

The biggest advantage that you are going to get with using the Bull Call Spread is because you widen up the spread, which is the same as saying that you increased the strike prices between these two options, you are able to choose to increase the amount of profit that you can earn. In addition, you can decrease the price, or decrease the number of strike prices that occur between your two calls, and then reduce your risks a little bit.

The biggest disadvantage that can come with using the Bull Call Spread strategy is that the time decay is definitely going to work against you. Even with a lower loss potential compared to some of the other strategies, if you see that the stock stays stagnant for too long, you will still close out the position with a loss. This is why it's so important to watch the market when you do this one. If you notice that it starts to stagnate, it may be time to exit the market and try a different trade to protect your investment.

With the Bull Call Spread, remember that you want to focus your energy on finding stocks that are seeing a moderate increase in price. You don't want to pick ones that are stagnating, ones that are going down, or even ones that have a quick rise in their profits or value. This one can take some time to make sure that you pick out the right stock. And you need to make sure that you move quickly, or have the stock keep going up rather than stagnating or reversing during

your time so that you can actually walk away
with a profit.

Chapter 8: The Ratio Spreads

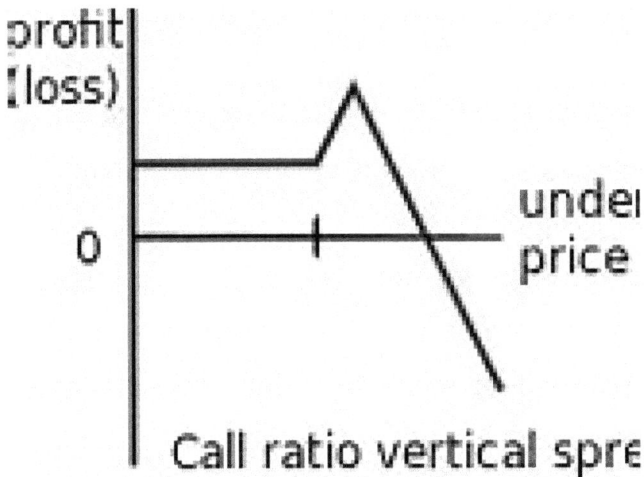

profit (loss)

0

under price

Call ratio vertical spre

And the final strategy that we will discuss in this guidebook is known as the ratio spread. There are many spreads that you can work with when you are an options trader, and we spent some time talking about a few of them. Most of these are going to fall into a specific category that makes it easier to know how they work. A ratio spread is a category for any spread that will involve buying and then selling different amounts on your contracts. This chapter is going to take some time to explore more about these ratio spreads and how you can use them in your trading.

The first thing that we need to explore are the steps that are needed to create a ratio spread. To start, a spread in options trading is going to be created when you purchase and then write contractions for options of the same type, and for the same asset, at the same time. You don't go through and buy at one time and then sell it later on; instead, you will do both at the same time so you are ready to go and get a profit when ready.

In most trades, you are going to purchase the same number of contracts as you write. To keep it simple, if you wrote out 100 contracts on the trade, then you would make sure that you purchased 100 contracts as well.

Things are a bit different when it comes to a ratio spread though. You will find that a ratio spread is going to involve you buying a different number of options compared to how many you write. There are different ratios that you can choose to go with, but the most common ratio is going to be 2:1. This would be 2:1 of contracts that are written versus contracts that are bought.

For the ratio above, if you wrote out 100 options on the trade, you would then need to purchase 50 options, from the same underlying asset, to get this ratio. You get the choice, based on the strategy you are going with, to use either puts or calls on these.

Now, there are going to be a few different ratio spreads that you can choose to go with. However, there are four main types that you can classify them as to make things a bit easier. The four main types that you may want to use for this include:

- Ratio back spreads: These are going to refer to any spread of this type where you will purchase more contracts compared to what you will sell.

- Diagonal ratio spreads: To create this kind of spread, you will need to sell the contracts, and then purchase a small amount of those contracts again. They need to be from the same type and have the same asset on them, and even the same price. But you will set the expiration date on the second group to be a bit later.

- Horizontal ratio spreads: This spread type is going to involve you selling your contracts, and then you will come back and purchase a smaller amount of them. They need to be for the same asset and you want to stick with the same strike price. But when you make the purchase, pick a later expiry date.

- Vertical ratio spreads: And the final option that you can go with here is the most common, and they are a vertical spread that you can work with. To create this kind of spread, you would need to sell your contracts before purchasing a smaller number of contracts of the same type. They should have the same expiry date and underlying asset, but you want them to come in with a different strike price to work properly.

Now that we have taken a look at that, it is time to look at how you would work with these ratio spreads. The main point of doing one of these spreads is so that a trader is able to get rid of any upfront payment when they are trying to take a position that is longer on your contracts. When you write out a higher number of contracts and then receiving a credit that is at least equal to, but hopefully higher than, the cost of the ones that you would like to buy, this can be successful.

If this works properly, it is possible to see some profits from this strategy regardless of whether the stock goes down, stays the same, or goes up. This is why they can be a very strong tool when you decide to use them in your options trading.

Let's take a look at an example of how you can use these ratio spreads and some of the ways that you are able to profit from doing this kind of strategy. We are going to start out by doing a purchase of an open order. You will need to purchase 100 of the below options contracts at a call of $200. The things you will need to remember for this one includes the following:

- Do the call
- Base it on the stock of your chosen company.
- The company you choose is going to trade at $50 right now.
- You want your strike price to be at $49
- Your ask price should be at $2.

After those are done, you will move over to doing a sell to open an order. You will write out 300 of the below options contracts, which in this case is going to give you a ratio spread of 3:1. This gives you $210 for a net credit of $10. The steps that you will do to make this one happen includes:

- Do the call
- Base the call on the stock that comes with your chosen company.
- The stock for that company is going to trade at $50.
- You want to set a strike price at $52
- Your bid price should be set at $0.70.

If you see that the price of the stock goes down and reaches the level of $48 by the date you chose for expiration, then the contracts you bought would expire without being worth anything, and you would lose out on your initial investment of $200. But, if the contracts that you wrote out also expire and are worthless, you will still receive $210 for writing them. This will make you a profit of $10 from that spread.

Now, there are times when the price of the stock will stay steady and when you reach the expiration date, it will still be worth $50. From here, you get the choice to exercise your option from the contracts you bough, gaining $1 per contract and earning a total amount of $100. As you paid $200 for these options, this is going to represent a loss of $100 for this part of the trade. But you also sold some of these as well and those earned you $210. If they expire as worthless, the spread would end up earning you a total of $110 in profit.

It is also possible for the price of the stock goes up to $52 by the time the contract expires, then you would be able to exercise the contracts that you bought for a gain of $3 on each of these, and that would earn you $300 overall. Since you paid only $200 for these, this means that this side of your spread is going to give you $100 in profits. The options you sold would earn you $210, but they expire as worthless, so you will earn a total of $310 on all this.

It is possible to lose in this if the stock price goes up quite a bit. So, let's say that the value of the stock rises to $56 by the time it expires, then you would be able to get $7 gain for each contract and you would earn $700 overall. You would then subtract the $200 that you had to spend to purchase those options, which would give you a $500 profit on this side.

But in this case, the options that you wrote would be exercised at a cost of $4 per contract, and that would total out to $1200. If you subtract the $210 that you got for writing them, this means that you would lose $990 on this side, which means that you lose out on $290 on this choice.

So, although you can use these kinds of ratio spreads to help profit from the security going down, up, or staying the same, there is still going to be a risk if you see that the price is moving in the wrong direction by quite a bit. If you would like to work with ratio spreads, you must make sure that you fully understand both the advantages and the downsides that could make you lose a lot of money on these trades as well.

To help reduce the amount of risk that you see with this kind of trade, you need to have a really good idea of the direction that the underlying asset is likely to take. You can look at a lot of past trends with the stock and pay attention to the way that the asset likes to behave. Lots of research and looking over charts, graphs, and other information can make a big difference. This can help you to determine the most likely course that the underlying asset will take over the time you hold the contracts. If you do this well, the ratio spread will be able to protect you, and you will be able to make a profit. But if you jump into this trading strategy too quickly and don't pay attention to what is going on with the market or with the stock, things are not going to work the way that you would imagine and you could still lose some money if your predictions are completely off.

Chapter 9: Reducing Your Risks When it Comes to Options Trading

Now that we know a little bit more about what options trading is all about and even some of the best strategies that you can use to see results with your trading, it is time to go through and learn some of the best tips and tricks that you can use in order to reduce the risks that you do better with your trades. While there is time to make some good profits with options contracts, it is going to contain some risks, just like any other type of investment. As a beginner, you want to make sure that you are able to keep your risks down as much as possible so that you can earn as much profits, without losing money, when you enter into your trades. Some of the ways that you can limit your risks as much as possible includes:

Know how to read the numbers

Reading the numbers can be one of the most difficult things when it comes to options trading. Understanding how much of one asset you should purchase, how many you need to write and sell, and everything in between can be confusing. Starting out small and building up as you gain more experience can be one of the best choices for seeing success in this kind of market.

If your brokerage firm allows it, consider doing a trial run of an options trade before joining the market. this is going to be a great way to help you learn more about the market, try your hand a few times with your strategy to see if you got the numbers down, and can really boost up your experience and your confidence level before you spend a lot of money. Not all brokerage firms will allow this, but if the one you chose does, it is really worth your time to give it a try.

Make sure that you pick a good strategy

We have spent some time looking at the different strategies that you can pick for options trading inside this guidebook. Some are great when the price of the underlying asset looks like it is going to go up. Some are great when the price of the underlying asset looks like it is going to go down. And some are best when there seem to be either high amounts of low amounts of volatility in the market. there are strategies that work with every market condition; you just need to know which one to use in each circumstance.

As you get more into trading, you will find that you will need to use a variety of different strategies based on how the underlying asset is doing. We talked about many different strategies and when you would want to use them. Making sure that you understand the best times to use each one, and actually using them in the right scenarios can make a big difference in how much you can earn in profits on those trades.

Learn all of the different terms that come with the market

One thing that can be helpful as you get into the market is learning all the different terms. We discussed a few of them at the beginning of this guidebook, but there are times when other terms may be important to know as well. Sometimes this is going to depend on which market you get into. Make sure to look up any term that doesn't make sense or doesn't sound familiar to you and work from there.

Find a mentor to work with first

Working with a mentor can make a big difference when it comes to how much you can learn in the beginning. A good mentor will be able to answer your questions, give you advice on how to do things in different market conditions, can talk about some of the different types of trades that they have done in the past, and so much more. This is a great source of information that can make your trading much easier.

If possible, it is best to work with someone who has actually spent time investing in the options market in the past. They understand more about how the different strategies work and can give you real life examples of what did and did not work for them in each situation. If you can't find someone who has directly worked in the options market, finding someone who has done the stock market, a broker, or another investing professional can make a difference.

One thing to note here is that, while it is a great idea to get advice from a mentor along the way, you need to take your own thoughts and research into consideration. The mentor is not going to intentionally steer you wrong, but it is never a good idea to just jump into a trade because someone else suggested it to you.

You must stop and think through all the different trades that you want to do. If someone gives you advice, stop and do a bit of research to see if that advice seems sound and if you should really stick with it or not. In some cases, you may find that the advice matches up and it works well to go with that, but other times you may decide to go a different route. It is your money at risk during the investment, so never leave it up to someone else on how you want to spend it.

Consider trading in the stock market first to get some experience.

If you have never spent time investing in the past, then you may want to consider some other forms first if you feel that options investing is going to be too difficult for you. Options trading does require you to do a lot of research and balance a lot of different contracts at the same time if you want to be successful. This can be a lot to take care of when you are first starting as an investor.

While options trading is a great way to make money and provides you with a variety of choices when it comes to how you would like to proceed, for those who have never invested in the market before, it all can be confusing. Starting out with a simple stock trade, without dealing with the contracts, can help ease you in. it shows you more about how the market works, teaches you how to do your research, often contains less risk than the others, and so much more. The choice is yours on how you would like to do this, but many find that starting with the stock market, which is often seen as easier, and then progressing to options trading can make things easier.

Leave the emotions at home

If you start letting the emotions get into your trades, then you are leading yourself right into failure on that trade. Emotions can be messy and often they allow us to stay in the market for far too long, compounding our losses more than ever. And, depending on the strategy you choose to go with for your trade, it is technically possible that your losses could be unlimited. To help protect your investment and your money, learn how to make smart decisions that will kick the emotions to the curb.

This is why it is such a good idea to come up with a sound strategy right from the beginning. This allows you the opportunity to have things laid out for you, steps on how to complete the strategy, and other tips that can make the trade easier to handle. If you are able to stick with the steps that come with your chosen strategy, and you don't let the emotions come into play, then you will do just fine with your trades.

Learn how to read lots of charts and graphs

You are never going to see success when it comes to working in options if you don't do your research first. Many beginner investors are just going to jump into the market and assume they know what they are doing without looking at any charts or graphs that are related to their chosen stock. But if you don't look at the history of the underlying asset, how are you supposed to pick the right strategy and make the right predictions to help you make a profit?

There is so much information that you are able to find within the graphs and charts, both of the market and of the underlying asset that you want to work with. You definitely need to take an in-depth look at them. But one benefit that comes with options trading is that, unlike traditional stock market trading, there are ways to make a profit no matter how the asset is doing.

Regardless of whether the asset is doing well and going up, whether it is volatile or not, or even if it is going down, you will be able to make a profit with the right strategy. If you would like to just pick one or two underlying assets to work with, you can experiment with the different strategies we discussed in this guidebook, along with different strike prices, lot sizes, and expiry dates, to find out just how easy it is to earn a profit no matter how the market is going.

Getting into options trading can be a different type of investment compared to what most people are used to. It brings about a lot of exciting investment opportunities that you just aren't able to find elsewhere, and the fact that you have the potential to make a profit no matter how the market is doing can be excited. Make sure to follow the tips above to help you to get the most out of this investment option while limiting the amount of risk you take on each trade as well.

Conclusion

Thank for making it through to the end of *Options Trading for Beginners*, let's hope it was informative and able to provide you with all of the tools you need to achieve your goals whatever they may be.

The next step is to pick which of the strategies that we talked about above will fit your needs when trading in the options market. Options can provide a unique opportunity to enter the market, and there are different strategies that work well no matter how a stock, or the market as a whole, is doing at the time. This guidebook explores seven of the best options trading strategies that you can use to really earn a great profit, even as a beginner. Whether you are looking to deal with a volatile market, a steady market, or even a market in a strong downtrend, you can use the strategies in this guidebook to help you see results with the trades you take on.

Finally, if you found this book useful in any way, a review is always appreciated!
Thank you so much for listening!

www.ingramcontent.com/pod-product-compliance
Lightning Source LLC
Chambersburg PA
CBHW060934220326
41597CB00020BA/3829